"Lovingly drawn by Aardman"

 Published by Ice House Books

© and ™ Aardman/Wallace & Gromit Limited 2019. All rights reserved.
Wallace and Gromit (word mark) and the characters "Wallace" and "Gromit"
© and ™ Aardman/Wallace & Gromit Limited.

Illustrations by David Lopez

Ice House Books is an imprint of Half Moon Bay Limited
The Ice House, 124 Walcot Street, Bath, BA1 5BG
www.icehousebooks.co.uk

ISBN 978-1-912867-19-6

Printed in China

LOVELY CHEESE GROMIT!

A CRACKING GUIDE WITH FACTS, RECIPES & JOKES

ICE HOUSE BOOKS

Cracking day trip, eh, Gromit lad?

CONTENTS

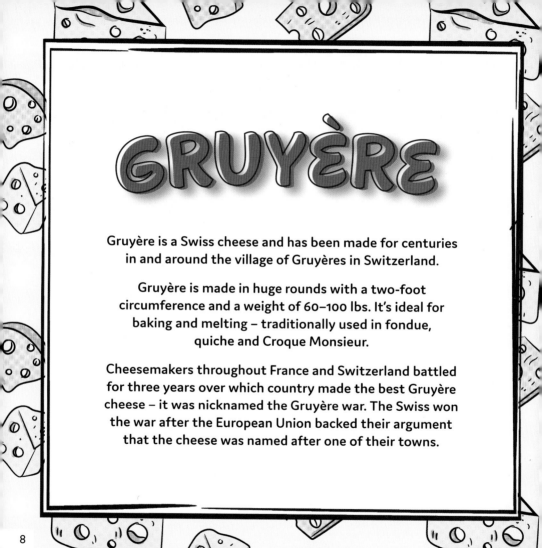

GRUYÈRE

Gruyère is a Swiss cheese and has been made for centuries in and around the village of Gruyères in Switzerland.

Gruyère is made in huge rounds with a two-foot circumference and a weight of 60–100 lbs. It's ideal for baking and melting – traditionally used in fondue, quiche and Croque Monsieur.

Cheesemakers throughout France and Switzerland battled for three years over which country made the best Gruyère cheese – it was nicknamed the Gruyère war. The Swiss won the war after the European Union backed their argument that the cheese was named after one of their towns.

A GUY THREW SOME CHEESE AT ME YESTERDAY.

HOW DAIRY!

BEER & GRUYÈRE FONDUE

Ingredients

240 ml (8.4 fl oz) pale lager
455 g (16 oz) Gruyère, shredded
1 tbsp cornflour
2 tsp Dijon mustard

dash of Worcestershire sauce
pinch of paprika
pinch of salt

Method

1. In a medium-sized saucepan, bring the beer to the boil over a medium-high heat. Once boiling, reduce the heat to medium-low so the beer is gently simmering.

2. In a bowl, toss the shredded Gruyère with the cornflour. Add the cheese mixture, one large handful at a time, to the beer. Stir the cheese in a figure-of-eight pattern and ensure it's melted before adding the next handful.

3. Stir in the mustard, Worcestershire sauce, paprika and salt.

Makes: 6–8 servings
Cook time: 10–20 minutes

4. Pour the cheese into a fondue pot and serve immediately. Chunks of bread, sausages and roasted vegetables taste great dipped into the oozy cheese!

12

13

STILTON

If you fancy making your own Stilton, you had better be living in Derbyshire, Leicestershire or Nottinghamshire, as it can only be legally made in these three counties using locally produced milk.

More than a million rounds of Stilton are produced each year. Blue Stilton is the most famous variety, with its blue veins and smooth, distinctive flavour. Its lesser known sibling, White Stilton, has a crumbly texture with a fresh, creamy flavour.

Blue Stilton is often eaten with celery, pears and crackers, or used to flavour vegetable soup.

WHICH HOTEL DO MICE STAY IN?

THE STILTON!

BROCCOLI & STILTON SOUP

Ingredients

1 tbsp sunflower oil
1 onion, chopped
1 litre (34 fl oz) vegetable stock
500 g (17.6 oz) broccoli, chopped

125 g (4.4 oz) mature Stilton
salt and pepper to taste
broccoli stems for garnish

Method

1. Heat a large saucepan over a medium heat. Add the oil and then the onion. Cook the onion for approximately 5–7 minutes or until it begins to soften.

2. Pour in the stock and bring the pan to the boil. Reduce the heat to a simmer and cover the pan for five minutes.

3. Remove the lid from the pan and add the broccoli. Bring the pan back to the boil and cook the broccoli in the mixture for approximately 4–5 minutes or until the broccoli is tender.

Makes: 4 bowls
Prep time: 10 minutes
Cook time: 25 minutes

4. Remove the pan from the heat. Crumble in half of the Stilton and mix. Purée the soup in a food processor (or with a stick blender) until it's smooth.

5. Season the soup with salt and pepper to taste. Pour it into four bowls and garnish with cut broccoli stems, then add the remaining cheese on top.

CHEESE HOLIDAYS

... EVERYBODY KNOWS THE MOON'S MADE OF CHEESE!

19

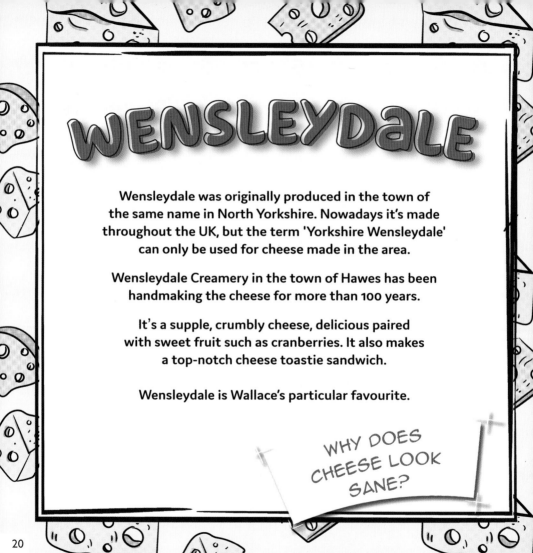

WENSLEYDALE

Wensleydale was originally produced in the town of the same name in North Yorkshire. Nowadays it's made throughout the UK, but the term 'Yorkshire Wensleydale' can only be used for cheese made in the area.

Wensleydale Creamery in the town of Hawes has been handmaking the cheese for more than 100 years.

It's a supple, crumbly cheese, delicious paired with sweet fruit such as cranberries. It also makes a top-notch cheese toastie sandwich.

Wensleydale is Wallace's particular favourite.

WHY DOES CHEESE LOOK SANE?

BECAUSE EVERYONE ELSE ON THE PLATE IS CRACKERS!

21

WENSLEYDALE TOASTIE

Ingredients

4 slices white or brown bread
25 g (0.9 oz) butter
100 g (3.5 oz) Wensleydale cheese

Method

1. Butter each slice of bread on one side. Arrange the Wensleydale on two of the slices of bread, buttered side down.

2. Cover your cheese-covered slices with the remaining slices of bread, buttered side up, to make your sandwiches.

3. Preheat a frying pan on a medium heat. Cook the sandwiches for approximately two minutes on each side until they're golden brown and the cheese has melted.

4. Cut your toasties into triangles and serve!

Makes: 2 servings
Prep time: 5 minutes
Cook time: 8–10 minutes

PARMIGIANO-REGGIANO

Parmigiano-Reggiano is an Italian hard cheese named after two of the provinces in which it's produced – Parma and Reggio Emilia.

It has been made for centuries in copper-lined vats from unpasteurized cow's milk, and is aged for an average of two years. It contains calf rennet so isn't suitable for vegetarians. The best version of this cheese has a sharp, complex fruity or nutty taste and a slightly gritty texture. Inferior versions can be bitter.

It's said that the playwright, Molière, loved this cheese so much that he asked for it on his deathbed.

ACCESS P
PORRIDGE
ATCH

SPAGHETTI BOLOGNESE

Ingredients

2 tbsp olive oil
400 g (14.1 oz) beef/veggie mince
salt and pepper to taste
1 onion, diced
2 garlic cloves, chopped

800 g (28.2 oz) chopped tomatoes
400 ml (14 fl oz) beef stock
400 g (14.1 oz) dried spaghetti
Parmigiano-Reggiano to serve
basil leaves to serve

Method

1. Heat a large saucepan over a medium heat and add a tablespoon of the olive oil. Once the pan is hot, add the mince and season with a pinch of salt and pepper. Cook on a medium-high heat until the mince is well browned, then transfer to a bowl and set aside.

2. In the same saucepan, add another tablespoon of olive oil and heat. Start by gently frying the onions with a pinch of salt for 5–7 minutes or until the onion has softened. Next, add the garlic and cook for two minutes.

Makes: 4 servings
Prep time: less than 30 minutes
Cook time: 30–60 minutes

3. Transfer your mince and any juices in the bowl back to the saucepan.

4. Stir in the tomatoes and ensure all of the ingredients are well mixed. Pour in all of the stock and bring the pan to a simmer. Reduce the temperature to a gentle simmer and allow the bolognese to cook for 45 minutes or until the sauce is thick and rich with flavour.

Continued overleaf...

5. Now cook the spaghetti according to the instructions on the packet.

6. Drain the spaghetti once it's cooked and add it to the pan with the bolognese sauce. Mix until the spaghetti is covered in sauce.

7. Serve in bowls topped with grated Parmigiano-Reggiano and fresh basil leaves.

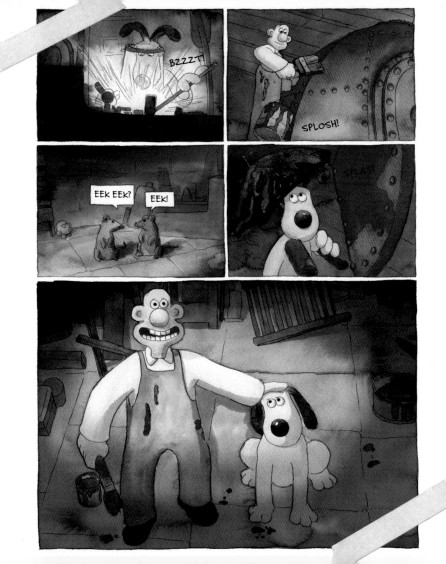

RICOTTA

It's thought that ricotta has been produced in the Italian peninsula since the Bronze Age! It's made from the whey that's left over from the production of other cheeses – its name literally means 'recooked'.

The milk whey used to make ricotta comes from no specific animal – it can be made from the milk of sheep, cow, goat or Italian water buffalo.

Ricotta's light texture and flavour – and the fact it can be beaten until smooth – makes it the perfect cheese to use in desserts such as cheesecake or pancakes.

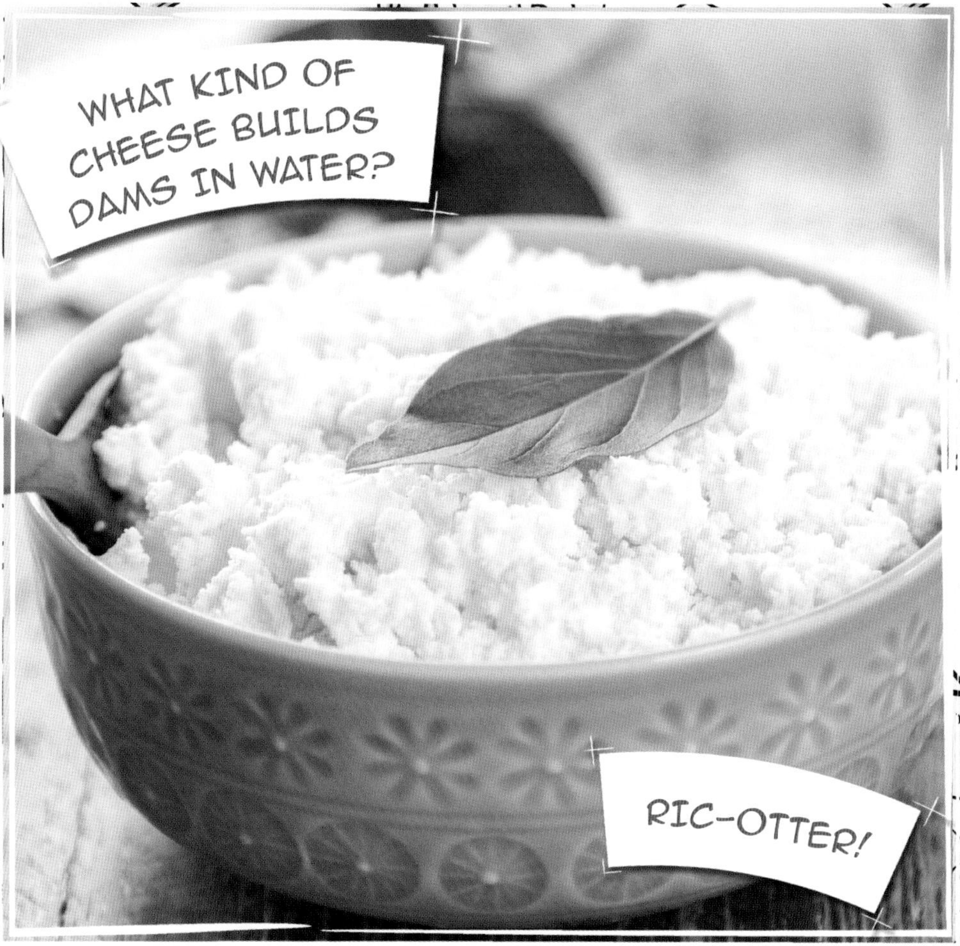
WHAT KIND OF CHEESE BUILDS DAMS IN WATER?
RIC-OTTER!

BLUEBERRY RICOTTA PANCAKES

Ingredients

2 free-range eggs
250 g (8.8 oz) smooth ricotta
120 ml (4.2 fl oz) freshly
squeezed lemon juice
2 tsp vanilla extract
120 ml (4.2 fl oz) milk

150 g (5.3 oz) self-raising flour
2 tbsp caster sugar
2 tsp baking powder
salt to taste
125 g (4.4 oz) blueberries
mint sprig for garnish

Method

1. Put the eggs, ricotta, lemon juice, vanilla extract and milk into a bowl and whisk them all together until they are well combined and smooth.

2. Sift the flour, sugar, baking powder, and a pinch of salt into the bowl and gently mix everything together until well combined. Note: the batter will be thicker than normal pancake batter. Gently fold in the blueberries.

3. On a low-medium heat, warm a non-stick pan and grease it with a small amount of butter.

Makes: 14 pancakes
Prep time: 15 minutes
Cook time: 15–20 minutes

4. Pour in some of your batter and fry it until it's golden, then carefully flip the pancake to cook the other side until that's also golden. Repeat this step with the remaining batter.

5. Once all of the pancakes are made, stack them and serve with fresh blueberries and a sprig of mint. You could also drizzle over maple syrup or sprinkle over some sugar for an extra-sweet touch.

GORGONZOLA

Made from unskimmed cow's milk, Gorgonzola is a beautifully stinky blue cheese from Italy. It has been made for centuries in the town of the same name in Milan.

Gorgonzola is typically aged for three to four months. The length of the aging process determines the consistency of the cheese, which gets firmer as it ripens. There are two varieties – Gorgonzola Dolce (also called Sweet Gorgonzola) and Gorgonzola Piccante (also called Gorgonzola Naturale or Mountain Gorgonzola).

This cheese is delicious melted into a risotto, used as a pizza topping, or served in a blue-cheese burger.

WHAT'S THE SADDEST CHEESE?

ACCESS PA

PORRIDGE HATCH

BLUE CHEESE

BLUE-CHEESE BURGER

Ingredients

4 seeded burger buns
4 beef or veggie burgers
salt and pepper to taste
olive oil

110 g (3.9 oz) blue cheese
(such as Gorgonzola Dolce)
red onion, tomatoes, lettuce
mayonnaise

Method

1. Preheat a cast iron skillet until it begins smoking, ready to cook the burgers.

2. Cut the burger buns in half, butter them and grill them, cut side down, for approximately one minute or until toasted. Set them aside for later.

3. Season the burgers with salt and pepper then lightly grease the cast iron skillet with olive oil.

4. Cook the burgers for around four minutes on one side, then flip them and add blue cheese on top of each burger. Cover the skillet with a lid and cook for a further three minutes for medium-rare (cook for a little longer if you prefer your beef well-done). If using veggie burgers, just cook until they're ready.

Makes: 4 burgers
Prep time: 5–10 minutes
Cook time: 10 minutes

5. Leave the burgers to rest while you slice your red onion and tomatoes.

6. Spread some mayonnaise on the burger buns and layer them with lettuce and tomatoes, add the cheesy burger and top with red onion.

7. Serve hot and enjoy!

CHEDDAR

Cheddar cheese is the most popular cheese in the world. It is made from cow's milk and originates from the English village of Cheddar in Somerset – where it has been made since the late 12th Century.

The name 'West Country Farmhouse Cheddar' can only be used for cheese produced from local milk within Somerset, Dorset, Devon and Cornwall using traditional methods. Anything else labelled 'Cheddar' can vary greatly in quality.

True Cheddar has a sharp, earthy flavour and is delicious paired with fruity, sweet chutneys such as pear and cranberry.

I'VE GOT AN ADDICTION TO CHEDDAR...

... IT'S ONLY MILD THOUGH

45

CIDER MACARONI CHEDDAR

Ingredients

250 g (8.8 oz) macaroni
35 g (1.2 oz) unsalted butter
50 g (1.8 oz) plain flour
400 ml (14 fl oz) full-fat milk
100 ml (3.5 fl oz) dry cider

salt and pepper to taste
2 tsp Dijon mustard
75 g (2.6 oz) Cheddar cheese, grated
75 g (2.6 oz) Gruyère cheese, grated
fresh parsley for garnish

Method

1. Preheat the oven to 200°C / 180°C fan / gas 6.

2. Cook the macaroni in a pan of lightly salted water, according to the packet instructions.

3. Drain the pasta but keep two tablespoons of the cooking water in the pan. Put the pasta back in the pan and stir through the remaining water, then set it aside until later.

4. To make your cheese sauce, gently melt the butter in a pan and stir in the flour. Take the pan off the heat and gradually add the milk, stirring it in with a wooden spoon to make a thick, smooth sauce.

Makes: 4 servings
Prep time: 10–15 minutes
Cook time: 35 minutes

5. Once all the milk has been added, slowly add the cider and mix. Put the pan back on the heat, bring it to the boil and stir well.

6. Stir the Dijon mustard and the Cheddar and Gruyère cheeses into your sauce until combined, then season to taste.

Continued overleaf...

7. Pour the cheese sauce over the pasta then transfer to an oven-proof dish and top with more Gruyère cheese.

8. Bake in the oven for 20–25 minutes or until crispy and golden on the top. Garnish with fresh parsley to serve.

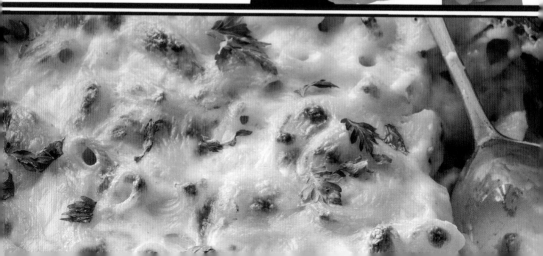

HALLOUMI

Halloumi is the squeakiest of all the cheeses!
Slices sometimes split while frying, which can make them
look like a pair of trousers (the Wrong Trousers perhaps).

Halloumi's unique salty taste and rubbery texture makes it
stand out from all other cheeses. It's a semi-hard, unripened
cheese made from goat's and sheep's milk – sometimes
cow's milk too. It is most closely associated with Cyprus,
where it has been produced for hundreds of years.

Halloumi's texture makes it perfect for grilling and
adding to salads, burgers and sandwiches.

WHAT DID THE CHEESE
SAY WHEN IT LOOKED
IN THE MIRROR?

ACCESS PA

PORRIDGE
HATCH

HALLOUMI!

HALLOUMI & MUSHROOM PITTA

Ingredients

2 tbsp olive oil
4 large flat mushrooms, sliced
pinch of salt
1 garlic clove, crushed
1 block halloumi, sliced

4 pitta breads
mayonnaise
1 red onion, sliced
roasted red peppers
rocket

Method

1. Heat a non-stick frying pan with one tablespoon of olive oil and cook the mushrooms for a few minutes with a pinch of salt, stirring frequently.

2. Add the garlic to the pan and cook until tender, then turn up the heat to boil off the moisture. Set the mushrooms and garlic aside and cover to keep warm.

3. In a separate pan, heat another tablespoon of olive oil and fry the halloumi on both sides until golden.

Makes: 4 pitta
Prep time: 5 minutes
Cook time: 10–15 minutes

4. While the cheese is grilling, chop your red onion and red peppers into strips.

5. Warm the pitta and spread some mayonnaise inside each one. Stuff them with all your fillings and enjoy!

CAMEMBERT

Camembert is a soft, creamy cow's milk cheese.
It is thought to have been invented by French farmer
Marie Harel in Camembert, Normandy, in 1791 – after she
received some advice from a priest from Brie.

Legally, Camembert must be left to ripen for at least three
weeks before it's packed and transported. This produces the
distinctive edible rind and creamy interior we all love.

It is said that Salvador Dali's painting, The Persistence of
Memory, was inspired by a melting wheel of Camembert.

WHAT'S THE BEST CHEESE
TO TEMPT A BEAR OUT
OF THE WOODS?

CAMEMBERT!

BAKED CAMEMBERT

Ingredients

2–3 tbsp sultanas
2 tbsp Port
1 whole Camembert

unsalted butter
crusty bread, toasted to serve

Method

1. Add the raisins and Port to a pan and heat over a high heat until the mixture is about to come to the boil. Take the pan off the heat and leave it to cool for around 30 minutes.

2. While the Port-soaked sultanas are cooling, preheat the oven to 180°C / 160°C fan / gas 4.

3. Prepare the Camembert by cutting a circular lid from the top, leaving a small border around the edge. Gently lift off the lid and scoop out the cheese with a teaspoon. Be careful not to damage the base or sides.

Makes: 1 to share
Prep time: 30 minutes
Cook time: 10 minutes

4. Spoon the Port-soaked sultanas into the cavity of the cheese, then spoon the cheese you've just removed on top and gently press it down so it fills the cavity. Pop the lid back on.

5. Cut a piece of foil big enough to wrap around the Camembert and lightly grease one side with unsalted butter.

Continued overleaf...

6. Tightly wrap the Camembert in the foil and fold over the edges to seal. Pop on a baking tray and bake for 10 minutes or until heated through.

7. Serve with slices of delicious toasted crusty bread!

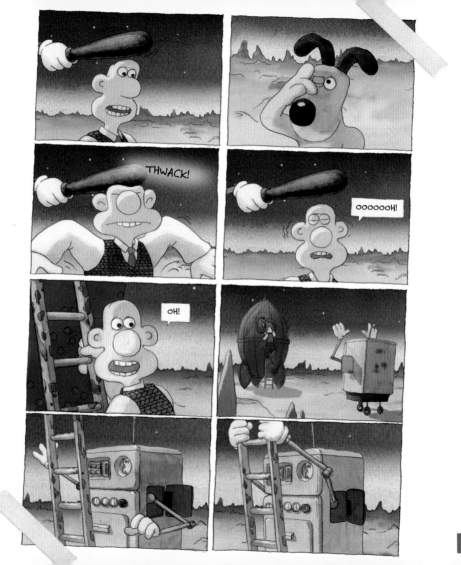